Breaking Free
Letting Go of False Identity Created by Satisfying the Needs of Others

Marietta Mills Jones

Breaking Free | Letting Go of a False Identity Created by
Satisfying the Needs of Others

BREAKING FREE A GUIDE TO HEALING, GROWTH, AND SELF-REDISCOVERY

Loving and caring for others is a beautiful gift, but when that love comes at the cost of your own well-being, it can leave you feeling lost, depleted, and disconnected from yourself. *Breaking Free* is a guide for those who have given so much to others that they no longer recognize the person in the mirror.

This book is not just about walking away, it's about reclaiming your identity, restoring your spirit, and rediscovering the power within you. Through practical exercises, reflective prompts, and thought-provoking insights, you will embark on a journey of self-healing and transformation.

Whether you have struggled with codependency, lost yourself in a relationship, or simply want to reconnect with your true self, *Breaking Free* offers the tools and wisdom you need to navigate the challenges of loving deeply while maintaining your own sense of purpose, joy, and authenticity.

Now is the time to reclaim your voice, honor your needs, and embrace the life you were meant to live. Let this guide be your companion as you step into a future of healing, growth, and newfound freedom.

Thank You

This book is dedicated to the village of extraordinary friends/family/my person, God placed in my life to walk with me on my personal journey to freedom. Your presence, love, and support have been invaluable, and for that, I am 4Ever Thankful!

TABLE OF CONTENTS

INTRODUCTION
THE COST OF LOSING YOURSELF

There was a time when I no longer recognized the person staring back at me in the mirror. The woman who once carried dreams, aspirations, and an unshakable sense of self had been buried beneath the weight of responsibilities, expectations, and the needs of others. Somewhere along the way, in my pursuit of being everything to everyone, I lost myself.

Like so many, I believed that self-sacrifice was an act of love. I thought that prioritizing my family, my spouse, my friends, even at the expense of my own well-being—was a noble calling. But what I failed to realize was that in constantly pouring into others without refilling my own cup, I was diminishing my essence. I became a version of myself shaped by the roles I played, rather than the truth of who I was.

The Formation of a False Identity

When we repeatedly put others first, we begin to shape our identity around their needs. We become the caregiver, the fixer, the supporter—until those titles define us more than our own dreams and desires. Over time, this false identity becomes a mask, hiding our authentic selves. We convince ourselves that as long as we're making others happy, we are enough. But at what cost?

The cost is waking up one day and realizing you don't know what truly brings you joy anymore. It's feeling lost in your own life, unable to answer the simple question: *Who am I beyond what I do for others?*

This book is about that journey, the journey of recognizing when you've lost yourself, reclaiming your worth, and redefining your life on your own terms. It's about peeling back the layers of who you thought you had to be and rediscovering the person you were always meant to be.

The Purpose of This Book

I wrote this book for anyone who has ever felt unseen, unheard, or forgotten in their own life. It is for those who have spent years prioritizing everyone else, only to wake up wondering, *What about me?*

In these pages, we will explore the warning signs of self-abandonment, the emotional and mental toll of living for others, and the steps needed to reclaim our authentic selves.

Together, we will walk through the process of:
- Recognizing the moments and patterns that led to losing ourselves.

- Reclaiming our identity, self-worth, and purpose

- Redefining our lives in alignment with who we truly are

This is not just a book, it's a guide, a mirror, and a roadmap back to you. You are not alone on this journey. And most importantly, you are worth finding again.
- Personal reflection on how you lost yourself in meeting the needs of others.

- How false identity forms when we prioritize others over ourselves.

- The purpose of this book: recognizing, reclaiming, and redefining who you are.

There was a time when I didn't know who I was outside of my role in someone else's life. I existed to fix, to support, to love, and to hold together what was falling apart. Somewhere along the way, my own identity became buried beneath the weight of someone else's needs.

Losing yourself doesn't happen all at once. It's gradual— one sacrifice, one compromise, one silent suppression at a time. When you spend years prioritizing others over yourself, you begin to wear a mask, a false identity that keeps you trapped in a cycle of approval-seeking, guilt, and emotional exhaustion. You become defined not by your own dreams and desires, but by what others need from you.

For those of us who have loved someone struggling with addiction, this reality is even more profound. We pour every ounce of ourselves into saving them, hoping our love will be enough to heal their wounds. But in the process, we lose sight of our own worth. The journey of breaking free is about more than just letting go of a toxic relationship or situation—it's about rediscovering who you were before the weight of others' expectations reshaped you. It's about stepping into the fullness of who you were always meant to be.

This book is for anyone who has ever felt lost in the shadows of someone else's needs. It is an invitation to reclaim your identity, to break free from the expectations that have kept your bound, and to finally embrace the freedom of being unapologetically yourself.

TIME OF REFLECTION – WHAT DID I LEARN

_____

_____

_____

_____

_____

_____

_____

_____

_____

_____

_____

_____

_____

_____

_____

_____

_____

_____

_____

_____

_____

_____

4EVER Thankfulie

CHAPTER 1
UNDERSTANDING THE FALSE IDENTITY

- What is a false identity?

- How it forms in relationships, caregiving, and codependency

- The emotional and psychological toll

What is a False Identity?

A false identity is the distorted self-perception that develops when individuals suppress their authentic selves in response to external pressures, relationships, or trauma. It manifests when people assume roles, behaviors, and beliefs that do not align with their true essence but are instead shaped by societal expectations, family dynamics, or the need for survival. This identity often emerges as a coping mechanism, creating a facade that protects individuals from rejection, criticism, or emotional pain. Over time, however, the false identity can become deeply ingrained, making it difficult to distinguish from one's true self.

How It Forms in Relationships, Caregiving, and Codependency

A false identity frequently takes root in relationships where validation, approval, or love is conditional. The desire to be accepted or needed can lead individuals to mold themselves into what they believe others expect of them. Three key areas where this occurs are:

1. Romantic Relationships – Many individuals lose themselves in relationships by prioritizing their partner's needs, desires, and expectations over their own. They may suppress personal ambitions, values, or even opinions to maintain harmony or

avoid conflict. Over time, this self-abandonment fosters resentment, emotional exhaustion, and a diminished sense of identity.

2. Caregiving Roles – Whether caring for a sick spouse, aging parent, or a loved one struggling with addiction, caregivers often neglect their own well-being. They may define their worth through their ability to care for others, resulting in self-sacrifice that erodes their individuality. This martyrdom mindset can make it difficult for caregivers to acknowledge their own needs without feeling guilt or shame.

3. Codependency – In codependent relationships, individuals derive their self-worth from being needed or fixing others. They often internalize a belief that their identity is tied to their role as a rescuer or enabler. This dynamic leads to a cycle of self-neglect, emotional suppression, and dependency on external validation, making it hard for them to function independently.

The Emotional and Psychological Toll

Living within a false identity takes a profound emotional and psychological toll. The consequences include:

- Emotional Suppression – Continually suppressing emotions to please others can lead to anxiety, depression, and a profound sense of emptiness.

- Low Self-Worth – When identity is based on external validation, self-worth becomes fragile and dependent on others' approval.

- Burnout and Exhaustion – The pressure to maintain an inauthentic persona drains energy, often leading to physical and emotional burnout.

- Resentment and Frustration – Over time, sacrificing personal needs for the sake of others can lead to bitterness and inner conflict.

- Identity Crisis – Losing touch with one's authentic self creates confusion about who they truly are, making self-discovery and personal growth challenging.

Conclusion

Understanding and acknowledging the false identity is the first step toward reclaiming authenticity. By recognizing how it forms and the toll it takes, individuals can begin to dismantle the roles they have assumed and reconnect with their true selves. The journey to self-awareness, healing, and self-acceptance is crucial for breaking free from false identities and embracing a life of genuine fulfillment.

TIME OF REFLECTION – WHAT DID I LEARN

_____

_____

_____

_____

_____

_____

_____

_____

_____

_____

_____

_____

_____

_____

_____

_____

_____

_____

_____

_____

_____

_____

_____

_____

_____

_____

_____

4EVER *Thankful.ee*

CHAPTER 2
THE ROLE OF CONDEPENDENCY

- How addiction (yours or a loved one's) distorts identity.

- The need to feel needed and its consequences.

- Breaking the cycle of codependency

How Addiction (Yours or a Loved One's) Distorts Identity

Addiction does not exist in isolation; it is a force that reshapes the lives of everyone it touches. When a loved one struggles with addiction, it can consume those around them, shifting priorities, values, and even self-perception. The desire to help, support, and protect can unknowingly lead to a loss of personal identity. Instead of being an individual with dreams, goals, and aspirations, a person caught in codependency becomes an extension of the addict's struggles.

The distortion of identity happens gradually. At first, it may seem like love, loyalty, or even responsibility. The caretaker role takes precedence over personal needs, and self-worth becomes tied to the well-being of the addicted loved one. It can become difficult to distinguish where one person ends and the other begins. Over time, personal goals, friendships, and self-care fade into the background, leaving behind a life dictated by addiction's chaos.

The Need to Feel Needed and Its Consequences

Codependency often stems from an innate need to feel needed. For many, being the one who "saves" or "fixes" the addicted loved one provides a sense of purpose and value. This dynamic can be deeply ingrained, sometimes originating from childhood experiences or past relationships where love was conditional upon service and sacrifice.

However, this need to be needed has serious consequences. It can lead to emotional exhaustion, resentment, and an inability to set healthy boundaries. The more codependent individuals give, the more the addicted person may take, reinforcing a cycle of dysfunction. Instead of helping, the codependent role can unintentionally enable destructive behaviors, allowing addiction to continue without accountability.

Additionally, the emotional toll of codependency can manifest anxiety, depression, and physical health issues. The constant stress of managing another person's addiction can deplete mental and emotional reserves, leaving little room for self-care or joy.

Breaking the Cycle of Codependency

Recognizing codependency is the first step toward breaking the cycle. Self-awareness allows for the acknowledgment that one's sense of worth should not be solely dependent on another's well-being. Healing from codependence involves:

- Establishing Boundaries – Learning to say no and recognizing that setting limits is an act of self-respect, not selfishness.

- Prioritizing Self-Care – Reconnecting with hobbies, friendships, and passions that bring joy and fulfillment.

- Seeking Support – Therapy, support groups, and trusted friends can provide guidance and encouragement on the journey to reclaiming identity.

- Letting Go of Guilt – Understanding that stepping back does not mean abandoning a loved one; it means allowing them to take responsibility for their own choices.

- Embracing Individuality – Rediscovering personal values, goals, and dreams that may have been lost in the shadow of addiction.

Breaking free from codependency is a process, but it is possible. By reclaiming personal identity and prioritizing self-worth, individuals can heal from the grip of addiction's collateral damage and step into a life of wholeness and fulfillment.

TIME OF REFLECTION – WHAT DID I LEARN

_____

_____

_____

_____

_____

_____

_____

_____

_____

_____

_____

_____

_____

_____

_____

_____

_____

_____

_____

_____

_____

_____
_____
_____
_____
_____
_____
_____
_____
_____
_____
_____
_____
_____
_____
_____
_____
_____
_____
_____
_____
_____
_____
_____
_____
_____
_____
_____

CHAPTER 3
THE TURNING POINT - RECOGNIZING THE NEED TO CHANGE

- Signs that you have lost yourself.

- The moment of realization: stories of breakthrough

- The first step toward rediscovering self

Signs That You Have Lost Yourself

Losing yourself in a relationship, a role, or an addiction—whether yours or someone else often happens gradually, like a slow erosion of your identity. The signs may not be obvious at first, but when you pause and reflect, they become undeniable. Here are some key indicators:

- Neglecting Your Own Needs: You find yourself constantly prioritizing someone else's well-being over your own, even to the detriment of your physical, emotional, or mental health.

- Loss of Joy in Personal Passions: The things that once brought you happiness, hobbies, interests, and dreams—no longer seem to fit into your life or feel worthwhile.

- Emotional Exhaustion and Burnout: You wake up feeling drained before the day even begins, weighed down by the emotional labor of carrying someone else's struggles.

- Lack of Boundaries: Saying no feels impossible, and you allow toxic behaviors to persist, justifying them out of love, fear, or obligation.

- Diminished Self-Worth: You begin to doubt your value, basing your worth on how much you can do for someone else rather than who you truly are.

- Social Isolation: Friends and family who once formed your support system start fading from your life, either because you have withdrawn or because they don't recognize the person you've become.

- A Constant State of Anxiety: You are always on edge, anticipating the next crisis, argument, or disappointment, living in a cycle of fear rather than peace.

Recognizing these signs is the first step toward reclaiming yourself. Often, the turning point comes when one moment of clarity breaks through the fog of self-sacrifice and reveals the urgent need for change.

The Moment of Realization: Stories of Breakthrough

Breakthrough moments often come in the quietest of whispers or the loudest of wake-up calls. Sometimes, it's a single event that shakes you awake. Other times, it's a gradual recognition that enough is enough. Here are a few stories that illustrate the power of realization:

- The Mirror Moment: One woman, who spent years supporting a spouse battling addiction, described looking in the mirror and not recognizing her own reflection. The vibrant, ambitious person she once was had been replaced by someone tired, broken, and unfamiliar. That moment prompted her to seek help and reclaim her identity.

- The Friend's Honest Words: Another person's turning point came when a longtime friend said, "I miss the old you." The simple yet profound statement cut through the denial and made her acknowledge how much she had changed—and not for the better.

- The Health Scare: For one individual, the wake-up call came in the form of a doctor's warning. Years of stress, neglect, and emotional turmoil had taken a physical toll, and a health crisis made it clear that if she didn't choose herself soon, she might not have a choice later.

Each breakthrough moment is unique, but they all share a common thread—the undeniable recognition that life cannot continue on its current trajectory. These moments are painful but necessary catalysts for transformation.

The First Step Toward Rediscovering Self

Realizing that change is necessary is powerful but taking that first step can feel daunting. The key is to start small and remain consistent. Here are some initial steps to help you begin your journey back to yourself:
- Acknowledge and Accept: Admit to yourself that you have lost pieces of who you are. Acceptance doesn't mean blame—it means recognizing where you are so you can move forward.

- Reconnect with Your Inner Voice: Spend time in silence, journaling, or meditation to tune in to your thoughts, dreams, and desires that have been buried under years of neglect.

- Seek Support: Whether it's therapy, support groups, or trusted friends, surrounding yourself with people who see you and support your healing is invaluable.

- Set Small Boundaries: Start with one small no. Protecting your energy is not selfish; it is necessary.

- Reintroduce Joy: Revisit an old hobby, listen to music that once moved you, or take a solo trip to rediscover what makes you feel alive.

- Prioritize Self-Care: Whether it's physical health, mental well-being, or spiritual nourishment, making time for yourself is a non-negotiable part of healing.

The road to rediscovering yourself is not linear, but every step forward is a victory. Your turning point is just the beginning of a journey toward self-love, resilience, and renewal.

TIME OF REFLECTION – WHAT DID I LEARN

_____

_____

_____

_____

_____

_____

_____

_____

_____

_____

_____

_____

_____

_____

_____

_____

_____

_____

_____

_____

_____

_____

_____

_____

4EVER _Thankful llc_

4EVER *Thankful*

CHAPTER 4
BREAKING FREE - THE PROCESS OF LETTING GO

Breaking free from a false identity is not just about recognizing that you have lost yourself, it is about actively shedding the layers of expectation, guilt, and obligation that have kept your bound. It is a process of unlearning old patterns, releasing emotional ties that no longer serve you, and reclaiming the power that was always yours.

Letting go is one of the hardest things you will ever do, not because you are weak, but because you have spent so much time believing that holding on was the only way to survive. You have built your life around the needs of others, and the idea of stepping away—of choosing yourself—can feel both terrifying and foreign. But true freedom comes when you allow yourself to release what is not meant for you, even if it means stepping into the unknown.

Understanding What You Are Letting Go Of

Letting go to is not just about walking away from toxic relationships or unhealthy situations. It is about releasing the beliefs, habits, and fears that have kept you trapped in a cycle of self-neglect.
You are letting go of:

- The need to prove your worth through self-sacrifice.

- The guilt that tells you prioritizing yourself is selfish.

- The belief that loves requires suffering.

- The fear of being alone or abandoned.

- The idea that you must meet others' expectations to be valuable.

This process is not about becoming someone new—it is about returning to yourself. It is about stepping into the person you were before life conditioned you to believe that your value depended on how much you could endure.

Releasing Emotional Attachments

Letting go to is not just a physical act—it is an emotional and mental process. Even when you recognize that certain relationships, roles, or habits are unhealthy, you may still feel emotionally attached to them. You may wonder if you are making the right choice, if you are being unfair, or if things could change if you just tried harder.
These doubts are normal. Your mind will resist change because it is wired for familiarity, even if that familiarity is painful. This is why breaking free requires a conscious decision to stop clinging to what is hurting you.

To release emotional attachments:
- Acknowledge your feelings—Grief, fear, sadness, and even relief are all part of the process. Allow yourself to feel them without judgment.

- Challenge the guilt—Remind yourself that letting go is not abandoning someone; it is choosing to honor yourself.

- Reframe your mindset—Instead of focusing on what you are losing, focus on what you are gaining: peace, freedom, and the ability to live on your own terms.

Detaching with Love

If you have spent your life being someone else's caretaker, rescuer, or emotional anchor, detaching can feel cruel. But detachment is not about shutting people out—it is about creating space for yourself to heal and grow.

Loving someone does not mean losing yourself to them. Detachment allows you to love and care without being consumed. It allows you to support others without sacrificing yourself. It means recognizing that you cannot save or fix anyone, and that your worth is not dependent on someone else's well-being.

Detaching with love involves:
- Setting clear boundaries that protect your emotional health.

- Allowing others to take responsibility for their own actions and consequences.

- Accepting that you cannot control or change people—only they can do that for themselves.

- Letting go of the need to be the savior or fixer in relationships.

Overcoming the Fear of the Unknown

One of the biggest barriers to breaking free is the fear of what comes next. When you have built your identity around others, stepping away can feel like stepping into emptiness. Who are you without the roles you played? What will your life look like now?

The truth is, you may not have all the answers yet, and that's okay. Letting go does not mean you must have everything figured out, it simply means you are choosing to trust yourself. You are choosing to believe that you are capable of building a life that is not defined by pain, obligation, or self-denial.

Fear of the unknown is natural, but it does not have to keep you stuck. Instead of viewing uncertainty as something to fear, see it as an opportunity. The space you create by letting go is space for something new, something healthier, something fulfilling, something that truly belongs to *you*.

The Power of Choice

At the heart of breaking free is one simple truth: *You have a choice.* For so long, you may have believed that you had no other option but to keep sacrificing, keep enduring, keep pleasing. But that is not true. You have always had the power to choose yourself—you just needed to realize it.

Choosing yourself means:
- Saying *no* without guilt.

- Prioritizing your own needs and desires.

- Walking away from relationships and situations that do not honor you.

- Refusing to shrink yourself to make others comfortable.

- Creating a life that reflects your truth, not someone else's expectations.

Letting go is not a single act; it is a journey. There will be moments of doubt, moments of temptation to return to old patterns, moments where you feel lost. But each time you choose yourself, you reinforce your commitment to freedom. Each time you let go of something that no longer serves you, you make space for something better.

And one day, you will wake up and realize that you are no longer bound by the weight of the past. You are no longer trapped in the identity that others placed upon you. You are free.

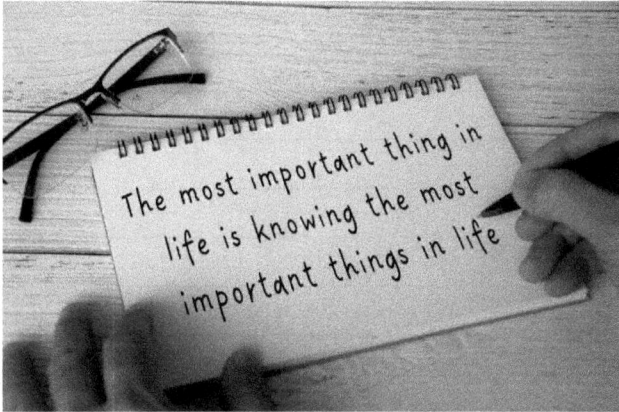

The most important thing in life is knowing the most important things in life

This is your moment. This is your life. And for the first time, it truly belongs to *you*.

TIME OF REFLECTION – WHAT DID I LEARN

_____

_____

_____

_____

_____

_____

_____

_____

_____

_____

_____

_____

_____

_____

_____

_____

_____

_____

_____

_____

_____

4EVER *Thankful uc*

4EVER Thankful

CHAPTER 5
RECLAIMING YOUR TRUE SELF

The journey to reclaim your true self begins with rediscovery — uncovering the parts of you that were lost beneath years of self-sacrifice, obligation, and the desire to please others. For so long, you may have measured your worth by how much you gave, endured, or accommodated. But now, it's time to ask:

Who am I when I'm not defined by what I do for others?

Rebuilding your identity is not about starting over; it's about reconnecting with your authentic self — the person you were before life's pressures caused you to shrink, silence your desires, or lose sight of your own dreams.

Rediscovering Your Identity

For those who have spent years caring for others or constantly putting themselves last, rediscovering your true self can feel unfamiliar — even overwhelming. But this is an opportunity to reconnect with your deepest desires and personal truth.
Start by reflecting on who you were before, the demands of life caused you to push your own dreams aside. Ask yourself:

- *What excites me?*

- *What activities make me lose track of time?*

- *If I had no obligations to anyone else, how would I spend my day?*

These questions guide you back to the passions, hobbies, and goals that once ignited your spirit. Exploring new experiences, revisiting old interests, or engaging in creative outlets can help reignite your sense of purpose. Your identity is not defined by what you give to others — it's shaped by what brings you joy, fulfillment, and meaning. Embrace this period of exploration as an opportunity to uncover what lights you up inside.

Facing Fear and Guilt

Letting go of an identity built around self-sacrifice can feel disorienting. After years of defining yourself by what you do for others, prioritizing your own needs may feel selfish or wrong. Guilt may whisper that you're abandoning those who relied on you, while fear may convince you that change will cause rejection or conflict.

But these feelings are natural — and they are signs that you're stepping into new territory. Growth often feels uncomfortable at first, especially when it means challenging long-held beliefs.

Understand that caring for yourself doesn't mean you're neglecting others; it means you're creating a healthier, more balanced version of yourself — one that can offer love and support without losing your own identity. By choosing yourself, you're giving others permission to do the same.

Setting Boundaries and Redefining Relationships

As you embrace your authentic self, some relationships may shift. Those who benefit from your selflessness may struggle to accept your new boundaries. But boundary-setting is not about shutting people out — it's about protecting your peace and defining what is healthy for you.

Learning to say no is an act of self-respect. Establishing emotional, physical, and mental boundaries allows you to reclaim control over your time, energy, and well-being. Ask yourself:

- *What behaviors am I no longer willing to tolerate?*

- *What expectations or demands no longer align with my values?*

- *Who uplifts and respects my growth — and who resists it?*

Surround yourself with people who celebrate your evolution. While some relationships may naturally fade, the connections that remain will be stronger, more authentic, and rooted in mutual respect.

Healing the Inner Child and Embracing Self-Compassion

Many of the patterns that shaped your false identity were formed in childhood. If you were taught that love had to be earned through sacrifice or that your value was tied to pleasing others, those beliefs may have followed you into adulthood.

Healing your inner child is a powerful step in reclaiming your true self. This involves offering yourself the love, care, and affirmation that you may not have received when you were younger. Speak kindly to yourself, forgive past mistakes, and nurture your emotional well-being.
When old wounds resurface — moments when you feel unworthy, anxious, or afraid — remind yourself: *I am enough just as I am.*
Embracing self-compassion allows you to move forward without the weight of shame or regret. Growth isn't linear, and setbacks are part of the process. The key is to extend yourself the same grace and patience that you would offer a loved one.

Building Confidence and Living Authentical

Confidence doesn't come from perfection; it comes from consistency. Every time you choose yourself — whether by speaking your truth, establishing boundaries, or taking steps toward your goals — you strengthen your sense of self.
To build confidence in your new identity:

- Speak your truth: Stop apologizing for your needs, feelings, and desires. Honor your voice and trust that your truth is valid — even if others don't always understand.

- Enforce your boundaries: Each time you uphold a boundary; you reinforce your worth and show yourself that your well-being matters.

- Celebrate your progress: No matter how small the step is, recognize your growth. Every choice that honors your authentic self is a victory.

With time, these actions build a solid foundation of self-trust — empowering you to live boldly, without shrinking to fit the comfort of others.

Creating a Life That Reflects Who You Are

Now that you're free from the expectations that once defined you, it's time to build a life that aligns with your truth. Living authentically means making intentional choices that reflect your values, passions, and goals. Ask yourself:

- *Does this choice align with my values or am I doing it out of obligation?*

- *Does this relationship support my growth or pull me back into old patterns?*

- *Am I pursuing what genuinely fulfills me — or what others expect from me?*

By consciously shaping your life around what matters most to you, you reclaim your power as the author of your own story — one built on authenticity, freedom, and self-love.

Embracing the Freedom of Being Yourself

The greatest gift you can give yourself is the freedom to exist as you are — without guilt, without apology, and without the need for external validation.

You do not have to earn love by sacrificing yourself. You do not have to prove your worth by being everything to everyone. You are enough — simply because you exist.

Reclaiming your true self is an act of courage. It means choosing yourself unapologetically, embracing your individuality, and stepping into the fullness of your identity with confidence and pride.

As you walk this path, remember:

You were never truly lost. Beneath the layers of expectation, fear, and self-sacrifice, you were always there — waiting to be seen, heard, and embraced.

Now, you are free Now, you are you!

TIME OF REFLECTION – WHAT DID I LEARN

_____

_____

_____

_____

_____

_____

_____

_____

_____

_____

_____

_____

_____

_____

_____

_____

_____

_____

_____

_____

_____

_____

_____

_____

CHAPTER 6
WALKING IN YOUR NEW FREEDOM

Breaking free from a false identity and reclaiming your true self is a monumental achievement—but the journey doesn't end there. True freedom isn't just about letting go of the past; it's about actively creating a future that reflects your authentic self. Walking in your new freedom means learning how to live without the crutches of people-pleasing, self-sacrifice, and codependent behaviors. It's about embracing a life where your worth isn't tied to how much you give to others, but it is rooted in the unwavering truth that you are enough just as you are.

Practical Steps to Maintain Your New Identity

When you've spent so much of your life fulfilling the expectations of others, it can be tempting to slip back into old patterns. Freedom is a choice you must make every day, and it requires intentionality.

One of the most important steps in maintaining your new identity is staying self-aware. Regular self-reflection helps you recognize when you're making choices based on your own desires versus when you're slipping into old habits of seeking external validation. Journaling, meditation, and quiet moments of introspection can help you stay grounded in your truth.

Surrounding yourself with people who respect and support your growth is also crucial. Some relationships may not survive your transformation, especially if they were built on unhealthy dynamics. Letting go of relationships that no longer serve you is painful but necessary. Seek connections with those who uplift you, encourage your independence, and honor your boundaries.

Another key practice is learning to say no without guilt. The old you may have agreed to things out of obligation or fear of disappointing others, but the new you understand that saying no is an act of self-respect. The more you practice setting boundaries, the more natural it will become.

How to Handle Setbacks and Triggers

Freedom is not a straight path; it is a journey with twists, turns, and occasional setbacks. There will be moments when an old trigger resurfaces—a familiar voice that makes you question your worth, a situation that tempts you to fall back into codependent tendencies, or an overwhelming urge to seek approval. When these moments come, don't see them as failures. Instead, view them as opportunities to reaffirm your growth.

When you feel yourself slipping back into old patterns, pause and ask yourself:
- Why do I feel the need to respond this way?

- Is this decision aligned with my true self, or am I reacting out of habit?

- What would my healed, empowered self-do in this situation?

Self-compassion is key during these moments. Instead of beating yourself up for making a mistake, remind yourself that transformation is a process. Growth doesn't mean never struggling, it means recognizing when you're struggling and choosing to respond differently than before.

Building a Fulfilling Life on Your Own Terms

Walking in your new freedom is about more than just breaking free from the past—it's about stepping boldly into the future you deserve. This is the time to reclaim your dreams, explore your passions, and build a life that truly reflects who you are.

Start by setting new goals based on what *you* want, not what others expect from you. Whether it's pursuing a career change, picking up a new hobby, traveling, or simply learning to enjoy solitude, give yourself permission to create a life that brings you joy.

Rediscover what makes you feel alive. What excites you? What are the things that bring you peace? Learning to listen to your own needs and desires is a skill that takes time to develop, but it is the foundation of living freely.

Most importantly, embrace the present moment. Too often, we spend so much time looking back at what we've lost or worrying about the future that we forget to enjoy the *now*. Walking in your freedom means allowing yourself to fully experience life, to find joy in the little things, and to appreciate how far you've come.

Stepping into Your Power

Your journey to freedom has been hard-won, but now, it is yours to claim. No longer bound by the weight of others' expectations, you have the power to write your own story. There will be moments of doubt but remember you have already proven your strength. You have already broken free.

This chapter is about stepping fully into your power—unapologetically, boldly, and without fear. Walking in your new freedom isn't just about avoiding the past; it's about embracing the limitless possibilities of your future. And the best part? It's a future where you get to be fully, beautifully, and authentically *you*.

TIME OF REFLECTION – WHAT DID I LEARN

_____

_____

_____

_____

_____

_____

_____

_____

_____

_____

_____

_____

_____

_____

_____

_____

_____

_____

_____

_____

_____

_____

_____

_____

CONCLUSION
YOUR JOURNEY TO WHOLENESS

- Encouragement for the journey ahead

- A final call to embrace your true self unapologetically

Throughout this journey, we have uncovered the deep and often painful reality of losing oneself in the needs and expectations of others. We explored how a false identity forms, how codependence takes root, and how the fear of letting go can keep us trapped in cycles of emotional exhaustion and self-neglect. But more importantly, we have learned that breaking free is possible.

The process of reclaiming yourself is not easy. It requires unlearning years—sometimes decades—of conditioning. It demands courage, self-reflection, and a willingness to walk away from relationships, habits, and mindsets that no longer serve you. But the reward is *freedom*, the ability to live authentically, without apology, and without the need for external validation.

What We Have Learned

1. Your identity is not defined by others. For too long, you have measured your worth by what you can give, fix, or endure for others. But your true identity is not found in self-sacrifice is found in self-discovery. You are not just someone's caretaker, rescuer, or emotional anchor. You are a person with dreams, desires, and a purpose beyond the roles you have played.

2. Codependency is not love. Love does not require losing yourself. Real love is mutual, respectful, and life-giving—not a one-sided commitment where your needs are always secondary. Understanding this is key to breaking free from toxic patterns and rebuilding healthier relationships in the future.

3. Letting go is not failure, it is freedom. Walking away from unhealthy attachments does not mean you have failed. It means you have chosen yourself. Letting go is an act of strength, one that allows both you and the other person to take responsibility for your own paths.

4. Healing is a journey, not a destination. There will be moments of doubt, grief, and even regret. But each step forward, no matter how small, is a victory. Healing is not about perfection—it is about progress.

Next Steps: Living in Your New Freedom

Now that you have begun the process of breaking free, the journey of maintaining your newfound freedom begins. Here's how you can continue moving forward:

- Practice Self-Reflection Regularly. Journaling, therapy, or quiet moments of introspection will help you stay connected to yourself and recognize when old patterns start creeping back in.

- Set and Maintain Boundaries. You have worked hard to reclaim your space. Protect it. Learn to say no without guilt and recognize that boundaries are a form of self-respect, not selfishness.

- Surround Yourself with Supportive People. Healing does not happen in isolation. Build a community of people who encourage, uplift, and respect you for who you truly are—not just for what you can offer them.

- Reclaim Your Joy. Rediscover the passions, hobbies, and dreams that were once buried under your responsibilities to others. Find what makes *you* happy and pursue it without hesitation.

- Give Yourself Grace. There will be days when you struggle, when doubt whispers that you should go back to the familiar. When that happens, remind yourself of how far you have come. Every step forward is worth celebrating.

This is your moment. The past does not define you. The expectations of others do not confine you. You are stepping into a life where *you* get to decide who you are, what you want, and how you choose to live. The journey to reclaiming yourself is not about becoming someone new, it is about returning to the person you were always meant to be. And that is the greatest freedom of all.

YOUR PATH TO FREEDOM!

_____

_____

_____

_____

_____

_____

_____

_____

_____

_____

_____

_____

_____

_____

_____

_____

_____

_____

_____

_____

_____

_____

_____

4EVER Thankful

4EVER *Thankful uc*

4EVER Thankful

ABOUT THE AUTHOR

Marietta Mills Jones is a beacon of inspiration, an advocate for personal growth, and a testament to overcoming adversity. Marietta's holistic approach to personal transformation addresses spiritual, emotional, and practical challenges. She openly shares her vulnerabilities, setting a powerful example for others on a similar growth journey.

Marietta's impact extends beyond her spiritual role to include authorship, motivational speaking, and philanthropy. Her collaboration on the books "*In My Own Words*" and "*Married to an Addiction*" have both won awards and reflect her commitment to sharing life wisdom. Marietta's extensive portfolio demonstrates her dedication to empowering a broader audience.

Recognized on various media platforms, Marietta's public speaking presence has included appearances on "Antigua Barbados Today" TV Show and "Battered Bruised Not Broken" Podcast Episode 7, which garnered over 1K viewers across the US and West Africa. She has also been featured in esteemed national publications. Marietta's compelling speaking engagements inspire audiences in conferences, churches, and community events, where she passionately shares messages of resilience, gratitude, and faith.

At the heart of Marietta's journey lies the reminder that authenticity, resilience, and story-sharing lead to true purpose. Online fundraisers through 4Ever Thankful, LLC, have successfully raised over $5000 for non-profits.

As the CEO of 4Ever Thankful, LLC, Marietta provides a comprehensive range of services designed to inspire and empower. 4Ever Thankful offers inspiring publications, dynamic workshops, personalized coaching, and tailored business solutions that foster gratitude, resilience, and lasting growth.

Guided by 1 Thessalonians 5:18, 4Ever Thankful, LLC is committed to helping individuals and businesses to embrace gratitude in all aspects of life, creating positive change and strengthening communities.

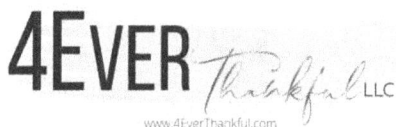

4EVER *Thankful* LLC
www.4EverThankful.com

4EVER *Thankful*

www.ingramcontent.com/pod-product-compliance
Lightning Source LLC
Chambersburg PA
CBHW070817280326
41934CB00012B/3203